101 Essays to Empower You to The Winning Edge

Frank Agin
Founder & President
AmSpirit Business Connections

ISBN: 978-1-967521-20-3

Published by:
418 Press, A Division of Four Eighteen Enterprises LLC
Post Office Box 30724, Columbus, Ohio 43230-0724

The Winning Edge

Acknowledgement

In sincere appreciation of Lewis Howes.

My *LinkedWorking* co-author, who provides enduring inspiration, and continually acknowledges my (albeit small) role in helping him.

The Winning Edge

Table of Contents

Look For These Other Books in This Series

101 Essays to Empower You to Rise & Thrive
101 Essays to Empower You to Up Your Game
101 Essays to Empower You to Build Momentum
101 Essays to Empower You to Limitless Reach
101 Essays to Empower You to Elevate Your Influence
101 Essays to Empower You to Peak Performance
101 Essays to Empower You to Live Unstoppable
101 Essays to Empower You to Achieve Greatness
101 Essays to Empower You to Break Barriers

Introduction

This book comes from the insight and creativity of Frank Agin.

Who is Frank? He is the founder and president of AmSpirit Business Connections, an organization that empowers entrepreneurs, sales representatives, and professionals to become successful and gain more referrals through networking.

He is the author of several books, including Foundational *Networking: Building Know, Like and Trust to Create a Lifetime of Extraordinary Success* and *The Three Reasons You Don't Get Referrals*. See all his books and programs at frankagin.com.

Finally, Frank shares information and insights on professional relationships, business networking and best practices for generating referrals on the Networking Rx podcast.

In the summer of 2018, he started planning this short-form podcast. As he mapped out what he wanted to bring to an audience of entrepreneurs, sales representatives, and professionals, he knew he'd have hundreds of programs.

But in addition to all that content, Frank noticed he also had a plethora of other materials—instructive, insightful, and inspirational. All this additional content was worthwhile, but none of it was long enough to create a full episode of Networking Rx.

Not wanting the material to go to waste, Frank developed it into short essays—approximately 150 words each. Then he started to record and share those segments daily under the brand Networking Rx Minutes.

For years, he shared a daily message of empowerment, intuition, and hope. This is a compilation of 100 of those essays. Enjoy.

-1-
Who Is Well Connected?

If you're looking to build your network, there are two basic approaches. The first is to get out there and meet lots of new people. That'll do it.

Of course, not every person you meet will work out. Not everyone will want to become part of your world. And you will find that some will only do so because they are looking to sell to you. So, this first approach is akin to kissing a bunch of frogs hoping to find the prince.

The second approach is to network through the people you already know. This works too and it's much more efficient. Think about it. The people you know already like you and have your best interest at heart. They are going to introduce you to the so-called princes and spare you the pain of the duds.

So, ask yourself, "Who do the people you know, know?" Chances are, they're connected to some wonderful people. So, work through your network.

-2-
Substance Not Form

Andrew Chiodo, in his book *The Fine Art of Networking*, states: "Effective networkers don't have to spend a hundred million dollars or look like a movie star, they just have to be honest, committed and EMOTIONAL about their offerings." Chiodo is right. Networking is not just about looking the part. It's about being.

It's not about doing things because you've calculated a sufficient return. Rather it's about sharing with others and showing up when you're needed simply because you have the capacity to do so.

It's not about saying things because they are just the right things to say. It's about saying things that are truly in your heart. It's not about just doing something because others are watching. It's about doing the right thing whether or not any one is there to witness it.

Building relationships and networking is not about pretenses. Rather, it's about being authentic. Networking is about substance and not merely form.

-3-
Tell Yourself a New Story

Cheryl Strayed, author of *Wild*, a chronicle of her hike on the Pacific Crest Trail, remarked that: "Fear, to a great extent, is born of a story we tell ourselves, and so I chose to tell myself a different story."

What story might you be telling yourself that has you locked in fear? Is it reasonable? Is it even likely? Chances are it's not. Chances are that the worst case scenario is highly unlikely. Chances are that nothing bad will happen at all.

So, stop yourself. Take a deep breath. And whatever situation is facing you, set about telling yourself a whole new story. Give it a positive ending. Better yet, give it a bold ending. One where you're the hero. One that gives you goosebumps.

Make the story that you tell yourself one that inspires you. One that makes you stand tall, push out your chest and take on the day!

-4-
Fail Forward

Do you want to achieve? Of course, you do. Everyone does. Do you want to know what the key to that is? Simple. Failure. It is. While that seems counterintuitive, it's true. Sure, succeeding is fun. But what do you learn? Little. With setbacks, however, you gain a ton (so much more than when you achieve).

Think about it. If everything always works out, how do you really know if you're stretching yourself? You don't. And, if that's all you ever did, you'd learn little and not advance beyond a comfortable plateau.

You're better to set lofty goals. Pursue unchartered ideas. And then grow from all the little snafus as you try to make it happen.

Dismiss the notion that successful people never fail. It's a myth. They fail often and learn much. Look at your life. Chances are that your biggest strides came right after a good kick in the head. So, get out there and fail yourself to success.

-5-
Learn from Master Networkers

Do you want to become really great at networking? Of course. Why wouldn't you?

Do you want to know the best way to get there? Read up on it? That's useful as there are lots of great books, blogs and newsletters on the topic. But it's not the best way. Find a webinar or training program? Again, that can be worthwhile as there are some good ones out there. But again, that's not the best way.

The best way to level up your networking and relationship building prowess is to find someone who is already successful and find out what they do.

So, answer this: Who is a great networker you'd like to emulate? Ask for 15 minutes of their time to share some advice on what to do. Also, as you see them at events casually watch how they interact. And get to know those who they know. This is the most effective way to become a master networker.

-6-
The Cure For Helplessness

Dr. Adam Grant, organizational psychologist at the Wharton School of Business and author of the bestseller *Give and Take*, shared on Twitter:

"When the world seems to be falling apart, it's easy to feel a loss of control. The best cure for helplessness is helpfulness. You might try a generosity day. Set aside an hour a week for people you can help and problems you can solve."

Grant's quote makes you think. Look around. At any point in time, there are people in need. People who have far less in material goods. And people who have far more in way of troubles.

Now think on your world. You've had down moments in the past. Maybe even today. And there are certainly more looming in the future. That's the nature of the human existence. There is occasional suffering.

You can ease your own suffering and quickly work through the pain of a setback by lending a hand to someone who has it worse than you.

-7-
Personal Versus Professional Relationships

Here's a question: What's one way you might build relationships in your professional life that you wouldn't do in your personal world? Can't think of anything? That's okay. It's a trick question. The reality is that how you build relationships should be no different in your professional and personal worlds.

Think about it. First, you only have one brain. And that glob of gray matter doesn't have a lobe for business activities and a separate one for your personal life. In either situation, your noodle churns away looking for clues to reveal that it's okay to build a solid relationship with a person. This is true whether the interaction is with a potential new boss or a prospective soul mate.

In addition, on any given day, when does your personal life end and your professional life begin? Clients and co-workers become lifelong friends. And vice versa.

In short, relationships are relationships. Thus, be consistent. Build relationships in your personal and professional lives in much the same manner.

-8-
A Language For All

Mark Twain, nineteenth century entrepreneur, humorist, and author of the famed tale *The Adventures of Tom Sawyer*, once said: “Kindness is a language that the deaf can hear and the blind can see.”

Twain is right. And further, it’s appreciated by every race, religion and nationality. Simply put, kindness is something that everyone on the planet values. Moreover, the appreciation of kindness has stood the test of time. And kindness will never go out of style.

The best thing about kindness is that it costs nothing and requires no unique skill to implement. Keep a smile on your face. Offer someone a compliment. Hold the door for others. Enjoy some small talk with a stranger. Pick up that stray piece of trash. Park just a little further from the door so others can have the prime spots.

Yes, kindness is a language for all, and it can be spoken at any time anywhere.

-9-
The Godness of 9/11

In her book, *The Light in 9/11: Shocked by Kindness, Healed By Love*, author Lisa Luckett shares a revelation:

"Amid the unprecedented tragedy of 9/11, an incredible beauty was revealed. It was made up of the strength and courage displayed in the struggle and the undeniable grace of the human spirit. People felt connected to one another. The unity and patriotism for our country was tangible. Compassion was everywhere. 9/11 was a great equalizer and the kindness it brought out in our collective experience was extraordinary."

"I call this the Godness of 9/11 (goodness with just one "o"). It is the incredible love, support and caring that always shows up in traumatic situations."

Luckett's words are inspiring. Godness. What a beautiful thing. But what if it didn't take shocking tragedy to bring it forth? What if you could just bring it forth on an ordinary day? How might that act of love ripple through your community and into the rest of the world?

-10-
Help Others Get What They Want

It's well established. It's almost a law of the natural world. But if you want more from the people around you, you need to find ways to contribute more to them.

As American author, salesman and motivational speaker "Zig" Ziglar was fond of saying, "You can get everything in life you want if you will just help enough other people get what they want."

So, if you haven't gotten everything in life you want, it's simply that you have not given enough to others. Think about it. If you've got big dreams – and you likely do – supporting others here and there might not be enough. It'll take more to get all you want.

What will it take exactly? Who knows? It's a mystery that only time can reveal.

Thus, you are left with a choice. You can accept less than you want or double down on helping others. What do you choose?

-11-
Dare To Ask

You do nothing alone. Your network is truly the source of all your accomplishments, achievements, and milestones. Knowing this, how can you tap into your network to obtain more or accelerate these successes? Simple: Just ask.

Despite this simple formula for advancement, you may be reluctant to ask, rationalizing that asking is an admission of weakness. Not true. Approaching others for assistance is a declaration of your desire to succeed.

Or you might be reluctant to tap into others because this could be an imposition on friends, relations, or business colleagues. Again, not true. The truth is that your network is both interested and eager to help you. The reason you don't get more assistance is because your friends, relations and business colleagues are not aware of what you need.

So, next time you are hesitant to ask, remember this: Your network doesn't fail you. Rather, you fail – you fail to make other aware of how they can assist you. So, dare to ask.

-12-
Invest In Happiness

Anger management coach and positive psychology specialist, Dr. John Schinnerer shared in his newsletter that, "*Happiness is a skill that can be learned and mastered.* It requires practice and commitment."

He then postulates, "Think of all the business books you've read this year. Now consider if you'd put the same amount of time and effort into becoming more content."

Science has demonstrated that humans are much healthier, more productive and have overall better lives when they enjoy a steady diet of happiness. So, doesn't it make sense to invest in your happiness?

The beautiful thing is that the journey can start at any point. Like right now. And this wonderful adventure to a better life can start with one single, simple step. Think of something wonderful in your life. That song you love. Your favorite coffee. That friend that always makes you laugh. Think about it and let that thought bring forth a smile.

There you go. You're on the road to happiness. Enjoy.

-13-
Little Touch Points

Successfully getting your name and message out is important. Actually, it's imperative.

The thing is that no one thing will do it. That is, no one thing gets others thinking about you. And no one thing will totally engrain you in the minds of others. Rather it's a series of little things that serve to get you on the minds of others. And, thereafter, it's an ongoing stream of those little things that will keep you there.

Little things, like: Taking the time to smile and say hello. Sending a handwritten note when others might opt for a pre-printed card. Forwarding website links with important information. Remembering important days and milestones, such as birthdays. Firing off a text or e-mail just because – totally void of any agenda.

These are all little things. None of them really carries a "wow' factor. However, each one serves to emblazon you in the minds of others just that much more. And it's these little touch points that make the difference.

-14-
The Character Column

In the 2008 NCAA Division II softball playoffs, the Central Washington Wildcats lost when a Western Oregon Wolves player hit a game winning home run. That's not unusual. That's the nature of sports. Winners and losers.

What was unusual about the loss is that player who blasted the home run severally injured her knee rounding first base. It was so bad she could not continue. But unless, somehow, she did the home run would be nullified.

In a show of great sportsmanship, Central Washington deliberately contributed to their own demise by carrying the fallen Western Oregon player around the bases to complete the home run.

Yes, Western Oregon notched a tally in the win column. And in sports winning matters. And while Central Washington may have taken the loss, it did so with a show of great integrity. In so doing, they notched a tally in the character column. And in business and life that matters most.

-15-
Attaining Greatness

In their book, *The 12 Week Year: Get More Done In 12 Weeks Than Others Do In 12 Months*, authors Brian P. Moran and Michael Lennington share this insight:

"Results are not the attainment of greatness, but simply confirmation of it. You become great long before the results show it. It happens in an instant; the moment you choose to do the things you need to do to be great."

They go on to explain that it's not winning an Olympic gold medal that makes the athlete great. Rather it's deciding to commit to do what it takes to operate at that level.

With this insight, greatness for you can literally happen in the next moment.

Committing to finally write that book.

Committing to complete a marathon.

Committing to do whatever it takes to successfully launch a business.

Sure, achieving these things will give you a fulfilled sense of satisfaction. But the moment you truly commit to see them through will serve to make you great.

-16-
Keeping the Conversation Rolling

In building relationships – whether you're working to solidify one you already have or kick-off a totally new one – small talk matters. It's the grease that keeps conversations flowing. And it's the gravity to pulls others to you.

But small talk is not always easy. You might not always be ready with a topic to ignite a conversation. And there are times when you feel like you've run out of things to say that will keep the conversation going.

When you hit this conversation wall, reach into your small talk arsenal for one of the easiest ways to start or keep a conversation going: Compliment the other person. Something like:

You seem to be in shape. What sorts of things do you do to stay fit?

That's a unique tie. Where did you find it?

I loved the short article you shared on social media. How do you find content like that?

An authentic compliment about their appearance, possessions or behavior enhances rapport, which serves to make conversation easier.

-17-
Life Is Difficult

In his 1978 bestselling book, *The Road Less Traveled: A New Psychology of Love, Traditional Values and Spiritual Growth*, M. Scott Peck begins with:

"Life is difficult. This is a great truth, one of the greatest truths. It is a great truth because once we truly see this truth, we transcend it. Once we truly know that life is difficult-once we truly understand and accept it-then life is no longer difficult. Because once it is accepted, the fact that life is difficult no longer matters."

Peck's quote is both accurate and inspiring. Life is difficult. Not all of it, but aspects of it. So what? It's difficult for everyone. Everyone. Starting and growing a business is difficult. Advancing a career is difficult. Meeting your litany of financial obligations? Difficult. There are difficulties to it all. Do you know what's also difficult? Not having a business, career, or possessions.

Life is difficult. It just is. Accept it. Once you do, the difficulty will disappear.

-18-
The New ABCs of Sales

International leadership change agent, award-winning speaker and podcast host Diane Helbig shared in her book *Succeed Without Selling*:

"Today the ABCs of sales are not 'Always Be Closing' but rather 'Always Be Curious.' When you are curious, you are thinking about someone else. You want to genuinely learn about the other person, the company, the situation."

"There is so much that is good about being curious. It relieves you of the feeling that you should be the one talking. Because, in all actuality, the opposite is true. You should be listening."

Helbig goes on to share that this curious state actually keeps you present and in the moment. And through this active listening you become more attentive, interested, and engaged. This serves to build the relationship which, in time, leads to more sales.

So, here's the deal: If you focus on being curious, you'll actually close more sales than when you focus on closing. Isn't that ironic?

-19-
The Power of Admiration

Understand this, when people discover that someone admires the qualities they possess, they tend to admire that person for their feelings in return. This is human nature hard at work. After all, it's all but impossible to be indifferent to or hold ill will towards someone who thinks you're pretty neat, right?

Knowing this, you can endear people to you by telling them what you admire about them. This is not hard to do, either. Think about it. Everyone has something admirable about them. Everyone.

People are smart. People are insightful. People are witty, if not outright funny. People are thoughtful. People are empathetic. People are good listeners. People are extremely articulate. And people can be a couple dozen other things beyond this.

Everyone has something admirable about them. And you can help build your relationships with others by simply reminding them of what you admire. Because once they learn why you admire them, they will admire you for something in return.

-20-
Networking Success By The Numbers

Aspects of life fall under three main headings "Easy," "Hard" and "Easier Said Than Done."

For example, weight loss is easier said than done. So is building wealth. And so is building a strong network. The issue relates to focus. In the short term it's relatively easy keeping track of calorie consumption, investment savings or interaction with your network. Maintaining any of these, however, requires ongoing attention.

The key to long-term success with any of these involves keeping score, as you tend to act upon that which gets measured. Track your calorie consumption and you'll lose weight. Examine your finances week to week and your wealth will build.

And to ensure that you network in a diligent and disciplined manner, you should somehow measure your ongoing networking activities. Adopt a system of giving yourself a tally for each event attended, hours involved in the community, or coffee conversations had. And as you focus on pumping up those numbers, your networking success will follow.

-21-
Network With H.E.A.R.T.

In the book *Becoming Competition Proof: Stand Out and Overcome Competition Through Generosity, Service and Added Value*, author and adventure coach Berta Medina offers a breakdown of action steps necessary when you're physically networking, using the acronym HEART. H-E-A-R-T.

"H" stands for Hello. Be the initiator. If there is someone in the room that you want to meet, simply walk up to them, and say hello.

"E" stands for Engage. Do yourself a favor and allow yourself to converse. Ask questions and give the person your undivided attention.

"A" stands for Amplification. Asking questions allows you to amplify their message to your network. So, be sure to inquire "How will I know if someone is a good referral for you?"

"R" stands for Relationship. This is the bottom line: What are you doing to establish a relationship with those you connect with?

And "T" stands for Time. Networking takes time. Results take time. Temper your expectations. Be patient.

In short, successful networking takes HEART.

-22-
Humble In Victory

You work hard, and as such hopefully achievement abounds. As it does, remember to remain as humble in victory as in defeat. Here are four thoughts to help you keep that mindset.

(1) Have Perspective: Put your achievement in perspective. While it serves to advance you, from an overall perspective it is likely small.

(2) Feel Compassion: Whenever you have an achievement, there is someone else on the other end. Reflect on their feelings and have compassion for them.

(3) Move Forward: One achievement does not give you ultimate success. As such, quickly resolve that you need to continue the pursuit of your next goal.

(4) Look For The Lesson: Every experience offers a lesson, so find it. Then use it to help you earn more accomplishments in the future.

By working through each of these four thoughts as you accomplish and achieve, you will not only impress others by your accomplishments, but they will also appreciate the humble nature with which you achieve them.

-23-
Leverage The Minds of Others

The world is complicated, isn't it? There are devices hitting the market every day that serve to make life easier. And seemingly every day there are software updates to improve on that improvement.

The rate of information and knowledge growth is overwhelming. Even with the topics upon which you focus, it's nearly impossible to keep up. You simply can't know everything.

But this is okay. It is. You can't know everything and, moreover, you don't need to know everything. That's not your responsibility. However, your responsibility is being willing to reach out to others.

This is part of the reason you have a network. You can tap into it to gather information you don't have. You can use it to get a sense of the vibe of others. You can use it to discover a fresh perspective on challenges that plague you. You've built a strong network. Now tap into it to leverage the minds of others.

-24-
Attune To Your Needs

Giving to others is a staple of building solid relationships. But it's also a great way to get things for yourself. Things like Information. Opportunities. Contacts. How do you do this?

Social architect Terry Bean has an answer. In his book *Be Connected: Strategies To Attract the Right Opportunities, Connections, and Clients Through Effective Networking* he shares, "As you give to others they feel almost obligated to give to you in return. This is the Law of Reciprocity. More importantly, when you give to them, they instinctively become attuned to your needs. Opportunities for them to help you, increasingly show up in their world."

As Bean implies, when you do for others, their minds almost immediately begin searching for things to bestow upon you. Even as they sleep, their brains churn away on that challenge.

So, you don't need to be too worried about how others will help you. Just focus on helping them. And trust their subconscious mind will do the rest.

-25-
Staying Current

Don't underestimate the importance of staying up on the news, weather, sports, and other current events. It's vital to good professional networking in a number of ways.

First, staying current puts you in position to add value to strategic partners. By keeping your eyes on the world around you, you're able to seize up information and opportunities that can really benefit someone you know.

Also, staying current allows you to engage in move conversations and keep the ones you typically have going. Think about it. Tidbits in the news, weather and sports gives you more 'arrows in your quiver' to keep small talk rolling.

Finally, staying current brands you as someone in the know. And being labeled as knowledgeable gives you more credibility whenever you speak. In addition, it heightens the degree to which you're considered a subject matter expert.

So, stay current. Read newspapers and magazines. Check the Internet. Listen to podcasts on recent happenings. It all serves to help build the relationships around you.

-26-
Share, Dare, and Care

People do business with those they know, like and trust. This principle is well established and is part of every program on building effective business relationships.

This principle, however, only speaks to the thoughts and feelings that others have towards you. It does not address the general actions you must take or attitudes you must have in achieving, as well as maintaining, this status.

Generally, to be known, liked and trusted, you need to Share, Dare and Care.

To be liked, you need to be eager to share. Referrals. Opportunities. Contacts. Information. And attention.

To be trusted, you need to be trusting. This entails being open and daring enough to reveal your goals and ask for help achieving them.

And through all of this, you need to care about others. Openly hope for the best. Celebrate their triumphs. Feel the pain of their setbacks.

In summary, whether you are known, liked, and trusted is a reflection of your actions and attitudes and not those of others.

-27-
Confidence Is Contagious

In his book *No One Gets There Alone*, mental edge guru and sports psychologist Dr. Rob Bell asks, "How do you know you can do something?" Then he answers, "When you see others do it."

As he implies, confidence is contagious. When you witness others having success it ignites your belief in yourself. Bell shared that he was inspired to run his first marathon on the heels of watching others complete the 26.2-mile run.

Look around. People are leaving corporate America and successfully starting their own businesses. You can too. People are publishing books. You could too. People are doing all sorts of things. And each is an indication that you could too.

So, what is your dream? What do you aspire to create, achieve, or accomplish? Figure that out. Then the next step for you is to find someone who's already done it. Get them on the phone or meet over coffee. Get reasonably close to them and catch the confidence that they have.

-28-
Thank The Four Percent

No doubt, you have a great business, and you serve most everyone well. Kudos. But like anything, it's not perfect. As such, from time to time you will let someone down.

Know this, however, statistics show that of those who have a problem with your product or service, only four percent will let you know. Only four percent! The other 96 percent won't say a thing to you. They won't share with you how you messed up. They won't indicate where you might be able to improve. But sadly, they just might tell others about your shortcoming.

So, the next time someone shares with you about a sub-standard experience they've had with your business, listen carefully. Don't make excuses. Certainly apologize. But mostly thank them.

Think about it. They've done you a wonderful favor. They've given you the means to fix something or improve. And that alone can help you retain the other 96 percent of potentially defecting customers and clients.

-29-
Follow Up on The Backside

If you're going to make the time to get out and network – you know, where you cast yourself amongst a sea of strangers and set about making them wonderful new contacts – then you should commit to following up with them after the initial meeting.

Remember, however you follow up – be it a handwritten note, an e-mail or a phone call – what you say should somehow reflect what you learned about them in your short time together.

But this is not always easy, especially if your memory is not great. After all, keeping straight all the details of even three or four new people can be a challenge.

Here is a tip to help you: Always carry a pen, so you can note important facts about them on the back of their business card. These don't need to be complete sentences. Develop a shorthand for yourself so you can briefly indicate notable things. This will jog your memory when craft your follow-up message.

-30-
The Case Against Pessimism

In his book *The Power of Optimism: Attitude Training for Those Who Want More From Life*, motivational speaker and leadership psychologist Tim Shurr shared about optimism by offering data he'd collected relative to those who are pessimistic.

Physically: Pessimists tend to be sick twice as much as optimists.

Mentally: Pessimists worry constantly, experience more feelings of guilt, and have a harder time saying no.

Emotionally: Pessimists tend to feel a sense of helplessness and often feel that they are victims.

Spiritually: Pessimists tend to feel more judged and feel as though external forces control their circumstances.

Professionally: Pessimists tend to make less money, procrastinate more often, miss deadlines and report job dissatisfaction.

As Shurr indicates, being pessimistic exacts a heavy toll on your life in lots of ways. So why would you be anything but optimistic about your situation. No, it's not perfect. No one's life is and no one suggests that it should be. But the glass is half full. Remember that.

-31-
Make Someone Laugh

Laughter, which is the productive result of humor, is a universal language. It is something that every culture or social class enjoys – there has never been (and likely never will be) someone who does not embrace a good chuckle. It will never go out of style.

Laughter can take away the deepest pain. And laughter can cut through the tensest of moments. And laughter serves to bridge any divide. Moreover, laughter forces you to see the wonder in your life.

While today's "politically correct" environment necessitates that you be careful with when and how you employ humor, this does not mean that you need to abandon it altogether.

Take the time and be open to finding good-natured humor to share – even if only off the cuff comments and one-liners. And be open to embracing the humor that others share. If you do these things, people will want to associate with you. So, go make someone laugh.

-32-
Decisions, Decisions

Teddy Roosevelt, conservationist, naturalist, writer, and 26th president of the United States is credited with saying:

"In any moment of decision, the best thing you can do is the right thing, the next best thing is the wrong thing, and the worst thing you can do is nothing."

Though Roosevelt spoke these words well over 100 years ago, the lesson is as valid today as it ever was. Every day you're faced with decisions. Some are monumental. Some are seemingly less consequential. But all are important to moving your life forward – personally and professionally.

Whatever the case, face up to these moments and endeavor to do the right thing based the information you have at that time and what your gut is telling you.

And as you do, don't be afraid of making mistakes. Odds are you will make a few. So what? It's part of the process. Learn from them and keep going. Whatever the case, don't do nothing.

-33-
Hiding In Plain Sight

In his book *The Science of Customer Connections: Manage Your Message to Grow Your Business*, marketing communication strategize Jim Karrh shares that the potential growth engine that is hiding in plain sight is everyday business messaging.

He goes on to share that almost universally business professionals are excited about the work they do. They get jazzed about the bells and whistles of a product or service. They marvel as to how small changes to variables can ripple through to massively impact the bottom line.

Then when it comes to articulating what it is or what it means, they either skimp, outsource, or altogether pass on sharing a message with others. It's as if they forgot or don't want to acknowledge that business is done with people and people need communication. And communication starts with an effective message.

Whatever you do, do it well. But also make effectively communicating with others something you do exceptionally well.

-34-
Goodness of Receiving

It's a mantra of life. One that's shared time and again, especially around the holidays. Everyone remarks, "It's better to give than to receive."

And this is true. Sure, getting something is fun. But giving is a heightened experience. Giving to others creates a feeling that carries you. Studies show that being generous with your time, talent and treasure makes your more productive and healthier, as well as the focus of admiration.

In summary, giving to others ignites a goodness inside you. But know this: Others want to experience this goodness too. Don't deny them. As such, a way that you can contribute to your network is finding ways that others can help you.

What have you gotten from your network recently? Big things or small? Referrals? New contacts? Information? Opportunities? The list could go on. Find ways that others can help you and politely share those things with your network. After all, it takes the goodness of receiving to generate the goodness of giving.

-35-
The 3-Foot Rule

Yes, many of the people you know were introduced to you by someone else. These connections serve to help fuel a growing and vibrant network. But a significant portion of your network develops from you connecting with and converting strangers into contacts.

You can ignite this organic growth by adhering to the "3-Foot Rule." This guideline simply states that anyone who is within three feet of you should be considered a potential candidate for striking up a conversation. And from this little chit chat a wonderful relationship can ensue.

As an added bonus, research shows that even brief conversations with these strangers can serve to make you happier and healthier. So, what excuse do you have?

Who's been in your 3-foot radius today? What did you say (or could you have said) that might have provided an opportunity for conversation? Think about it and prepare for your next encounter.

-36-
Ordinary Superpowers

In his book *Ordinary Superpowers: Unleash the Full Potential Of Your Most Natural Talents*, Mark Henson, founder of *sparkspace*, an award-winning business retreat center in Columbus, Ohio, unveils the meaning of Ordinary Superpowers as:

"The talents and skills that enable you to contribute at your highest levels, help the most people and experience the most fulfillment in life."

As Henson implies throughout his book, while the notion of Superman and Wonder Woman, with incredible powers of speed and strength, can make daydreaming fun, you are more than adequately equipped just the way you are.

That is, you have the ability to be a hero in your own special way. Maybe it's connecting people. Or perhaps communicating complex things in a simple way. Or deploying your special ability to listen empathetically.

So, whatever it is, put your hands on your hips, throw back your shoulders, and commit to saving the day in your own special way. Whatever the case, the world needs your ordinary superpowers.

-37-
Hand Over a Talking Stick

The notion of the talking stick originated from various native American tribes, included the Mohawk, Seneca, and Oneida, in what is now upper New York state near the shores of Lake Ontario.

The talking stick was an ancient and powerful communication tool. It dictated a code of conduct that ensured a level of respect to be followed during tribal gatherings. In short, the person holding the stick, and only that person, was designated as having the right to speak. All others were to listen quietly and respectfully.

Whether or not you're a native American, you can adhere to this notion of respect. When you engage another in conversation or participate in a meeting, figuratively hand over a talking stick when it's someone's opportunity to talk.

In so doing, you deem them to have an unfettered right to speak. Listen quietly. Listen respectfully. Wait patiently. Hear them thoroughly. They may never know what inspired you, but they will appreciate the respect you've given.

-38-
It's The Relationship, Stupid

James Carville was an astute political strategist who was instrumental in upsetting President George H.W. Bush's re-election bid and seating Bill Clinton in the White House.

Carville believed that election would hinge neither on moving speeches nor on debates over special interest programs. He believed that the election would hinge on one basic issue – the abysmal state of the U.S. economy.

Thus, to keep the Clinton election team focused on this basic issue he wrote on a dry erase board three simple words: "The economy, stupid."

Success in most everything – business, athletics, or the political arena – comes down to the basics, those fundamental elements or actions that, if in place and appropriately executed, generally guarantee success.

Networking is like anything else. You need to consistently execute on the basics to be successful. In networking, take a lead from James Carville and write on your dry erase board, your desktop blotter or on your screen saver three simple words: "The Relationship, Stupid."

-39-
Be a Card Counter

In the book *Becoming Competition Proof: Stand Out and Overcome Competition Through Generosity, Service and Added Value*, author and adventure coach Berta Medina-Garcia shares:

"If I attend a networking event with 5 people, I take 5 business cards. If I attend a networking event with 100 people, I take 5 business cards."

Medina-Garcia sort of makes you chuckle, but she also makes you think. She goes on to share:

"How many times do you attend a networking event and see people passing out their business cards like they getting paid to do it? You may take one out of politeness, then half-way through the event (since they don't remember you because they don't care), they offer you another. Don't be this person. They suck."

Medina-Garcia implies that your business card is not an advertising message that you need to spread far and wide. It's simply a means of further connecting you to someone you've just met.

So, be a card counter. But only count to five.

-40-
If It's Endurable, Endure It

Marcus Aurelius, a beloved emperor in what is termed the Golden Age of the Roman Empire, once remarked: "If it's endurable, then endure it. Stop complaining"

Building a business is hard. A successful career is hard. Life is hard. There are moments to celebrate, for sure. But there is lots of tough sledding in between. Long days leading into late nights. Two steps forward only to be followed by one-point-nine steps back. And the rules of play seem to unfairly change at the worse possible moment.

When you're in those tough patches, make Marcus Aurelius' words your mantra. You can make it through. So, do so. After all, bemoaning your situation will not change it. You're no longer a child, so whining will not cause some adult figure to swoop in and take your troubles away.

It's simply up to you. So, pin your ears back, put your head down and endure it.

-41-
What To Ask For

Know this: Your network does not fail you. Rather, you fail – fail to make friends, relations, or business colleagues aware of how they can assist you.

To avoid this failure, you need to determine what you hope to accomplish and then ask your network for assistance in fulfilling those ambitions. For example:

Ask a friend to give you an honest assessment of a marketing initiative you contemplate undertaking.

Ask current clients for names of prospects for your marketing list, or, better yet, referrals to close friends and contacts.

Ask satisfied clients to give you a raving online review. Ask business professionals to keep you apprised of opportunities of which you might take advantage.

Ask industry colleagues to keep you "in the know" on changes that might affect you.

Next time you are reluctant to ask of your network remember this: If you ask for assistance, you are guaranteed some chance of getting it. If you don't ask for assistance, you're guaranteed not to get it.

-42-
You Can't Sell Anything

International leadership change agent, award-winning speaker and podcast host Diane Helbig shared in her book *Succeed Without Selling*.

"In order to compete effectively, sales professionals and small business owners must be able to answer the question: Why do people buy from me?"

She goes on provide that answer: "They buy because they need or want what you have to sell, and they trust you can deliver relative to all aspects of the sale."

She continues with a counterintuitive point that "You can't sell anything to anyone." Rather, all you can do is build trust and be available with something they want, when they need it."

Helbig is implying the no one likes to be sold, but they enjoy buying things they want and need. So, if you are in business for the long-term, build relationships, create a quality offering, and establish trust. If you do, in time, the sales will come.

-43-
Sharing Good Seed

There was a farmer who consistently grew high quality, award-winning wheat. One year a local reporter interviewed him and learned that the man shared his seeds with his neighbors so they too could plant it in their fields.

Perplexed, the reporter asked why the farmer would share his award-winning seeds with those who are essentially his competitors, both in the market and at the county fair?

The farmer explained that "The wind picks up pollen and carries it from field to field. Thus, if my neighbors grow inferior wheat, cross-pollination will steadily degrade the quality of all the wheat, including mine. If I am to grow good wheat, I must help my neighbors."

This lesson is true of all aspects of life. If you want to have a successful life, you need to share seeds of success. If you want continued happiness, you need to share the seeds of happiness. With whatever you want, you need to share the seeds of it with others.

-44-
The Empowering Help-Seeking Style

To be successful, as you know, you need to add value to others. It's human nature. Those who take all the time eventually become shunned. But conversely, those who do nothing but give, in time, oddly impair themselves too.

So, if you do nothing but give you need to allow others to add value to you. And an important part of that is asking for the help you need.

When you ask others for help, instead of expecting them to generate the end-result for you, ask them to help empower you so that you can help yourself.

Think about it. You'd gladly teach someone to fish, if they asked. But you'd likely be hesitant to just give them one fish today because you know they'll likely be back for another tomorrow. And thus, you know your help is not lasting. So, ask for help that empowers you to do things for yourself.

Remember, an empowering help-seeking style is immensely more powerful long term as compared to one that essentially only seeks a quick fix.

-45-
Yes, And ...

On the *Networking Rx* podcast, guest Gina Trimarco, a sales consultant who uses improv comedy to help her corporate and entrepreneurial clients, shared about the second rule of improvisation – Yes, and...

She indicated that you should never rebut or defend against a prospect or networking partner's objection. Rather, you should accept the statement and build on it. You can do this by simply saying "Yes," restating the comment, and then adding to it.

Maybe a prospect states that your prices are high. You might not agree, but you shouldn't dispute it either. Rather, following the second rule of improvisation, Trimarco would coach you to say something like, "**Yes**, our prices are high, and for that we deliver substantially more value than any of our competitors."

So, instead of feeling confrontational with a rebuttal, you agree – pulling the prospect along. Then you take the opportunity to build on the value you offer.

Yes, this is insightful, and it works.

-46-
One For Dad

In October 2012, with minutes remaining in the game and a 20-plus point lead, St. Clairsville High School senior, Michael Ferns was racing down the sides for what appeared to be his fourth touchdown. On this night, no one was going to stop him from scoring.

Nevertheless, Ferns deliberately stepped out of bounds inches from the goal line. Everyone was confused. "Huh? What? Why?" The situation was inexplicable to all, except to Ferns and his coach. You see, 36 hours earlier teammate Logan Thompson's father had died of a heart attack. Despite his great sorrow, Thompson came to the game to support the team.

Ferns wanted to give up just another touchdown in a storied high school career so that Thompson could score just one in honor of his father. And on the next play that's what happened. And with that touchdown, there was a lesson too: Little things in your hands, can be immense in the hands of another.

-47-
Networking Refined

Some believe that successful networking depends on strong skills and techniques. And they are mistaken. Successful networking is about building solid relationships. And that involves habits and attitudes that serve to get those you know to like and trust you.

These relationship-building habits and attitudes will fall into one of three categories:

One is, presence, which involves those habits and attitudes that serve to cast a positive impression of you on others.

Another is, altruism, which involves the habits and attitudes associated with your selfless contribution to the world around you.

And, finally, there is integrity, which involves your habits and attitudes associated with whether your network perceives that you fairly interact with others.

Successful networking is about focusing more on the "your everyday thoughts and routines" and ignoring occasional tactical strategies. To be successful at this you need to surrender to the notion that you must refine your attitudes and habits to focus on building the relationship.

-48-
Pain As a Catalyst

In her book, *The Light in 9/11: Shocked by Kindness, Healed By Love*, author Lisa Luckett shares a revelation:

"Trauma is a shocking opener that projects you to an entirely new place. Pain is always a part of that. Pain gets our attention, and while it can be unpleasant and scary, it is also a natural and integral part of the human experience. As difficult as it might be, allowing pain, without avoiding, denying, or medicating it too much, can lead us on a fast track to personal growth."

Luckett implies that when something traumatic happens, instead of asking "Why is this happening TO me?", you should be asking "Why is this happening FOR me?" What might the Universe be trying to tell me? What is it that I am being shown? What am I supposed to learn?

If you take this approach to working through life's challenging events, you'll find that the pain can become a catalyst to a better future.

-49-
Inspire Others

Mike Krzyzewski, long-time head basketball coach at Duke University and the winningest basketball coach at any level, with well over 1,000 victories, shared on Twitter: "Good players inspire themselves; great players inspire others."

Coach K, having mentored literally hundreds of young men over forty-some years, has more than an adequate sample size to make this declaration about athletes. However, this proclamation is not limited to sports.

Pick any profession. Choose any career. Select any vocation. The individual who is committed to personal development and effectively leading themselves, does well. However, the individual who adds to that, helping raise up others around them does exceptional.

So, don't aspire to be just good. You can be so much more than that. Set your vision on greatness. Find ways to help others develop and effectively lead themselves. In short, inspire others and achieve excellence yourself.

-50-
Unleash Selflessness

Altruism, selflessness, generosity or whatever you want to call it, is not limited by your personal wealth. It's not limited by your professional experience. And it's not limited by your influence. Do you know what it's limited by? It's simply limited by your willingness to do something for another. That's it. Nothing more.

It's true. At any moment. In any place. You can do something for someone. It can be for a family member. It could be for a close friend. Maybe for a mere acquaintance. Or it could be for even a total stranger. Any one of these you can do something for.

You can make an introduction. You can share some information. You alert someone to an opportunity. You can give a compliment. You can lend an ear. You can make a random act of kindness. You can do these things and countless others.

But remember, it's all in your control. So, take a moment to unleash selflessness on another.

-51-
Brighten Someone's Day

As word-of-mouth referral consultant Matt Ward shares in his book *MORE: Word of Mouth Referrals, Lifelong Customers and Raving Fans:*

"There's almost nothing better than receiving a heartfelt compliment. It makes the person you are complimenting feel great and you can tell from their smile that you have brightened their day."

That said, it not always easy to find something for which you can complement another. Fortunately, Ward offers a tip for that. He shares: "Look at your contacts' social media feeds to discover what they are sharing and how they feel about their accomplishments."

He's right. Social media is a treasure trove of information about the people you know, any of which you can use to give someone a heartfelt compliment. With that potential accolade, you can do any number of things to deliver the compliment. For example:

Leave a message on social media. Share a handwritten note. Make a call. Or send a text.

Whatever the case, brighten someone's day.

-52-
Discover The Best in Others

Twentieth-century writer, William Ward had more than 100 articles, poems and meditations published in magazines such as *Reader's Digest* and *Science of Mind*. And as such, he was an often-quoted writer of inspirational truisms.

One such bit of sage advice was: "When we seek to discover the best in others, we somehow bring out the best in ourselves."

You see, when you see something admirable in another, your mind unconsciously searches for times when you have exhibited a similar quality. And whether or not an example is there, your mind subconsciously pushes you to bring about change to make it happen.

With that information, stop. Think about the people you know. Look at the people around you. Ignore their flaws. Look for the best in them. Humor. Selflessness. Confidence. Kindness. Whatever you find, know this: These qualities will soon reflect themselves upon you.

-53-
A Caring Ear

In a conversation, you should listen to what the other person is saying, right? That's intuitive. From there, an effective means of building the relationship is to then talk about what they are talking about. That is, follow their lead and don't steer the conversation somewhere else.

The more you focus on listening to what the other person sees as important to them, the more you make that topic important to you, too. And the more you learn how to connect through another person's way of seeing a situation.

It's counter-intuitive to think like another, sure. It unnatural. However, when you develop the skill to see life through the eyes of another, you create an environment that serves to attract people into your world.

More or less, when you focus on talking about what passionately or directly interests others, you give them more than just your attention. You actually give them a gift. The gift of a caring ear.

-54-
Service Before Vocation

In his book *Who Do You Need To Meet?* professional speaker Rob Thomas shared that "Networking is the most effective and successful strategy to acquire sales, customers and clients."

While most everyone agrees with that, few really know how to make it happen. Fortunately, Thomas goes on to offer further insight. He shares that you can make networking this successful strategy, but ... and this is key ... it's only successful if you "consider the other person's needs and goals before you even think about a sales process."

Thomas then goes on to elaborate that if you want networking to work for you ... really work for you ... in your interactions with others you need to put your vocation aside. Instead, listen to them for opportunities to help them in ways other than what it is you sell.

His mantra is "service before vocation." Focus on service. Then make what you do one of the last conversations you have.

-55-
Social Media Success Habits

To be a successful networker in the 21st century, you need to embark upon a degree of networking using specifically designed Internet websites. LinkedIn. Facebook. Twitter. Instagram. And if you want to be successful using social media, you need to adopt appropriate social media habits.

First, you should never dismiss someone because of the content of their profile or their stature in life. You just never know who they are connected to.

Next, for everyone that you connect with, ask yourself, "How can I help this person?" Then commit to acting. If you do, things will come back to you in spades.

Also, don't binge your social media activity. Rather, commit to taking consistent moderate action. Over time, you will be amazed at all that comes your way using this approach.

Finally, be patient. Using social media is like a slow cooker and not a microwave.

If you follow these simple rules, your online networking will add beautifully to what you do offline.

-56-
A Quality Affair

Generally, when people first embark on networking it's a "quantity over quality" game. That is, they set about meeting as many people as possible, gathering names and e-mail addresses to build a contact list.

From this some sort of content "drip" campaign is set in motion. You know, where a consistent flow of quasi-promotional emails is pushed to your inbox at an almost predictable pace. And all of this is done in hopes of saying the right thing, at the right time to land a client. Or a new project. Something.

But the reality is that you don't do business with inboxes. You do business with people. And people do business with those with whom they have a relationship. So, to successfully network, focus less on the quantity of contacts and more on developing solid productive relationships. Learn about the people you meet. Help them however they need to be helped. Act as if their success will one day be yours.

Remember, networking is not a quantity game. Rather it's a quality affair.

-57-
Correspondence Bias

In one of her recent weekly *Neuro Nugget* newsletters, neuroscience geek Melissa Hughes asked, "Can you think of a time that you waited for someone who was late thinking 'How rude!' or 'He must think his time is more valuable than mine!'?"

She then goes on to query, "Now think about the last time you were late for an appointment. What kind of excuse did you make? Traffic? An earlier meeting ran long? No parking spaces?"

Hughes explains that behavioral scientists refer to this as correspondence bias. It's the tendency to place greater emphasis on situational factors when considering your own behavior while placing greater emphasis on character or intention when considering the behavior of others.

Let's face it. You judge others on a black and white scale but judge yourself with a gray scale. It may not be right but it's human. That said, there's nothing to prevent you from taking a deep breath and tempering the shortcomings of others with a little grace. Remember, they're human too.

-58-
Standing Out

Imagine this: You've just walked into a networking event. It's the first time you've ever attended. It's absolutely huge. A sea of bodies milling about. Some you know. Most are total strangers. You don't want to be just another face in the crowd. No. Of course not. You want to stand out. Right?

Here's surefire way to do that: Promote others. Seriously. Meet someone new. Get to know them. Then introduce them to someone you know, talking each up as you do. Then go connect with someone else. Get to know them, then connect them to someone else. Do it again.

Quickly, you will brand yourself as a connector – that someone who is known to connect people to other people, information, and opportunities. And everyone is attracted to the connector.

Eventually, what you do will come out and people will want to help you too. But by helping others first, what you do will become more memorable.

-59-
A Daily Dose

There is little question that being healthy is something you either take for granted (if you're in good health) or something you long for (if you're not in good health). Either way, there are necessary steps to take to get and stay healthy. Clear mind. Pain free. And full of energy. Personal health is important.

Professional health is just as vital, right? When your business or career is firing on all cylinders, life is so much happier and worry free. And when this is not the case, you will move heaven and earth to get it back on track.

To maintain optimum professional health, the best prescription is a daily dose of networking. That is, everyday connect with someone. Anyone. It can be an old acquaintance. It can be somehow you don't know well. Or it can be a total stranger. It does not matter who; simply make the connection. Do this every day (weekends included) and you will maintain great professional health.

-60-
The Generosity Multiplier

In his book *Be Connected: Strategies To Attract the Right Opportunities, Connections and Clients Through Effective Networking*, professional speaker and social architect Terry Bean shared:

"Simply stated, the law of generosity says that 'as I do well by you, the universe is paying attention and will bend in ways to make sure good is done for me.'"

So, never question whether adding value to the world is a worthwhile endeavor. In reality, giving to others will always leave you receiving more in return than you put into the equation.

As Bean goes on to explain in his book, not only does the universe look out for you, but so does the person you've helped. So, in essence, whenever you add value to another in a meaningful and selfless way, there are two factions working to benefit you in return.

-61-
Center On Relationships

The tie that binds you to others is relationships. And these are forged over many years of interacting, familiar experiences, or perhaps common interests.

As an example, consider CNN's involvement in the Gulf War. It was not sheer luck that CNN was the only major news operation left in Iraq as the United States and its allies launched Operation Desert Storm. It was relationships.

You see, for years the station's founder, Ted Turner, had been providing periodic seminars for news organizations around the world at CNN's Atlanta headquarters. This allowed CNN, just a young upstart at the time, to develop relationships with its counterparts in the Middle East. These relationships were further developed when Turner traveled to the Middle East early in 1990.

It was these relationships that provided CNN correspondents with a safe haven in Baghdad and other parts of the Middle East while other major news organizations were on the outside looking in.

Knowing this, center your attention on developing relationships. Eventually, the benefits will come.

-62-
Success Is a Team Effort

You work hard. And you're strategic in your approach. It shouldn't be surprising that you and your team will realize more than your share of accomplishments. Congratulations.

As you look to celebrate your next accomplishment, remember that often a tremendous amount of time and energy is wasted trying to determine who should be anointed with the appropriate kudos on a particular achievement. You're best to not get caught up in this exercise.

You see, the reality is that with any achievement, everyone is entitled to some credit. Even though you might be the obvious champion of the win, it didn't happen alone. Behind you was a supporting cast of contributors. And then there are the people who shore up those efforts. And so on!

Therefore, no matter what milestone you achieve, some credit is due to those around you. You need to eagerly and energetically seek to distribute it. Remember that success, in all its forms, is really a team effort.

-63-
33 Milliseconds

The next time you approach someone at a social gathering or networking event, consider this.

According to Mark Given, author, speaker and innovator of the trust-based philosophy, "Studies at several well-known universities and prominent research groups show that you give your spouse, your friend, your kids, your boss, your colleagues, your teammates ... all those people you need every single day to survive and to thrive ... a whopping 33 milliseconds to one tenth of a second for them to show you that they are in an approachable mood."

He goes on to share that you judge the extent to which others are approachable by their body language, facial expressions, and an unseen aura of how they feel and how they might react to you.

This is the reality: Your mind operates that fast ... and so do the minds of others. Knowing this, if you want to be approachable, you need to consistently carry a vibe that you truly want others in your life. Or in less than a second, they won't be.

-64-
Stories Stick

In the 21st century, there is no shortage of messages bombarding us every day. Social media. Television. Radio. Billboard. Print. All of this makes it hard to rise above the noise.

So, if you really want to be memorable, share stories as part of your communique whenever you're giving a presentation, having a conversation, or just reciting your 30-second commercial.

Remember, stories captivate people's attention much more than sharing the same basic information, especially facts and figures. Furthermore, a story helps them relate what you're saying. And stories serve to stick in the memory better.

So, share stories as you communicate. They can be from your personal experiences. They can be from the experiences of others. They can even be just examples, as long as they're crafted from likely possibilities. These stories will make you more interesting, stick in the mind of others, and in time they will lead to more opportunities for you.

-65-
Bamboo Roots

The bamboo starts from a tiny, tiny seed. It's planted and watered. It's watered some more. And, well, nothing. After a year of being watered, still nothing. Same for year two. Another year passes and still nothing. The same is true of year four. Nothing. It's not until year five that the bamboo peeks its shy little head out of the ground.

At this point, amazing growth begins to happen. In just weeks, the bamboo will tower up to 90 feet or more. You see all those years that looked like nothing, there was really something. Underground, out of sight, the bamboo grew its roots deep. It was preparing a necessary foundation to support the amazing structure it would become.

The same holds true for you. Often hard work seems to go unrewarded. But like the bamboo, your efforts are forming a structure that an amazing future will rest upon. So, even if your efforts are never immediately rewarded, remember they always serves you like bamboo roots.

-66-
Be True to Yourself

In her book *Secrets To Becoming A Master Networker*, professional speaker and professional relationship expert Stacey O'Byrne shares "Networking is a skill; it's also an art. It is a skill because skills are developed and perfected. Networking is also an art because like all art of any modality, it involves finesse, authenticity, and a high level of congruency."

She goes on to acknowledge that while this might sound a little "woo woo," it's meant to. She shares that networking is about building relationships. And the best way to do so is by being yourself. And, as you know, being yourself is not something definitive.

Sure, you have an absolute height, weight, and eye color. But the characteristics that make up your personality are somewhat amorphous. While you might have a consistent overriding intent, the situations and circumstances that surround you are constantly changing.

O'Byrne's advice to tackle this is: "Be true to yourself and your plan will be true to you."

-67-
Box The Room

If you think about it, successful small talk is similar to boxing. Boxers choreograph their initial moves, generally making delicate punches, known as jabs. Their subsequent actions are determined by the opponent's response to these jabs.

Small talk relies on an analogous strategy. Your preliminary questions are verbal jabs. They should be simple to answer in a word or two. Then depending on the answers, you either follow up with another jab or look for an opening to pose a more in-depth question. A punch!

With the proper mental preparation, this becomes almost rhythmic:

What do you do? Jab!

How long have you done that? Jab!

That hasn't been that long. What did you do before that? Jab!

Interesting change. How did that transition occur? Punch!

So, next time you're headed to that business function or Chamber after-hours event, remember you are not there to work the room. You are there to box it. Jab. Jab. Jab. Punch.

-68-
Chains Of Habits

Warren Buffett, business tycoon, philanthropist, and one of the most successful investors in the world, once offered this cautionary remark on the notion of behavior patterns: "Chains of habit are too light to be felt until they are too heavy to be broken."

While it's true that the right habits serve to create the foundation for lasting and remarkable success, not all habits are achievement oriented. In fact, many can be downright destructive in nature.

As Buffett alludes, the problem is that these harmful habits can sneak up on you and become fixed before you realize it. And once they do, it takes a Herculean effort to break them.

To protect yourself, you should focus on building positive, success-oriented habits. One of those habits should be to consistently take a hard look at your actions as well as your inactions. By doing this you will guard against any behavioral pattern that could serve to chain you down.

-69-
13 Times

As Jonah Berger noted in his book *Contagious: Why Things Catch On*, only seven percent of word of mouth happens online. Yes, only seven percent. That's not even double digits.

Despite all the attention we pay to social media, a whopping 93% more word-of-mouth activities happen in the offline world. Face-to-face meetings. Telephone conversations. And even the written word.

So, to get your message out or effectively build your personal brand, social media alone will not cut it. Rather, take a hard look at what some might deem old-fashioned communication tactics.

In fact, judging by Berger's assertion, to be as effective as you'd like, you need to do upwards of 13 times more communicating and brand building outside the confines of the Internet than you do on it. So, turn off your computer. And pick up the phone.

-70-
Books To Millions

Starting in the 1970s, JB Fuqua donated almost $40 million dollars to Duke University. With these monies, the private university in Durham, North Carolina created an elite business school, and named it after its main benefactor – the Fuqua School of Business.

Here's the interesting part of the story: JB Fuqua, who made his fortune from a variety of businesses in various industries, never attended Duke University. He never even attended college. And he never lived in North Carolina. In fact, Fuqua grew up on his grandparent's tobacco farm in Virginia and built much of his business empire in the state of Georgia.

So, what was his tie to Duke University? As a teen, Fuqua educated himself reading borrowed books he received in the mail from the Duke University Library system. And he credited that system for his business success.

The lesson: Be generous. Even in a small way. You never know what good it will do. And you cannot predict what loyalty it will create.

-71-
Pizza Math

Let's talk pizza. Everyone loves pizza. Now, this is not about pizza styles, types, or preferences. This is about pizza math. Yes, pizza math.

Okay, think about this. If you get a 7-inch pizza, you are getting 38.48 square inches of deliciousness. But if you spring for a 14-inch pie, you get almost a whopping 154 inches of gut busting pleasure. That's a lot a pizza pie. And, whether or not you trust the math, the point is this: As the diameter of the pizza increases, the amount of pie you get grows exponentially.

And the same is true of networking. As the number of people with whom you develop great relationships grows, the potential benefits from your network - such as referrals, contacts, information, opportunities, etc. - grows exponentially.

So, a path to success is to focus on building solid relationships, whether you do it on the golf course, over coffee, or sharing a 14-inch pizza.

-72-
Sow Well; Reap Well

In his book *The Power of Optimism: Attitude Training for Those Who Want More from Life*, motivational speaker and leadership psychologist Tim Shurr shared a metaphor:

> "You are the farmer responsible for sowing your own field. The way I understand it, we have three choices: 1) Plant healthy seeds that will eventually develop into a hardy nourishing harvest; 2) Stick garbage in the ground and cover it with dirt; or 3) Do nothing with the field and see what happens."

Based on the options that Shurr provides, what sort of farmer are you? The answer is easy, right? It's almost rhetorical. You intend to plant healthy seeds, right?

While the answer is easy, what follows might not. Shurr goes on to share that the healthy seeds are the information and thoughts you put into your mind. What podcasts are you listening to? What books and articles are you reading? Who are you associating with? That is the sowing that leads to a great harvest.

-73-
Computing Network Value

How much social capital do you have? You know, social capital – the end result of your networking efforts.

Does the answer really matter? Perhaps not. But what is critical is knowing that the relative value is increasing from one year to the next. In his book, *Achieving Success Through Social Capital*, Wayne Baker provides insight about determining if the relative value is increasing via an examination of three simple questions.

First, how many people do you know? Not mere connections, but people you could call upon today and get a response.

Second, which of these people know each other? Your social capital is better positioned if there is less connectiveness amongst those you know.

And, finally, of the people you know, who do they know that you might not? This represents the potential growth of your social capital.

Sure, how much social capital you have is not important, per se. But it's vital that you always have a keen focus on enhancing it.

-74-
The Truth About Compliments

Giving someone a compliment can be an easy way of adding value to the world around you. And yet, the average person doesn't. According to research conducted at the University of Pennsylvania's Wharton School of Business there are two main reasons why people might not give more compliments.

First, people underestimate the positive impact that their compliments have on others. They perceive that the recipient of a compliment takes it in a ho-hum manner. However, research shows that receivers are completely uplifted by these accolades.

Second, people worry that stopping someone to share a compliment will be perceived as an intrusion. Again, the research shows that this is not the case at all. In fact, recipients seldom ever feel imposed upon when interrupted to receive words of validation.

So, what's stopping you? People love the compliments you give, and they will happily take the time to hear them.

-75-
Sur-Thriving

In her book, *The Light in 9/11: Shocked by Kindness, Healed By Love*, author Lisa Luckett shares that:

> "Life is not about just surviving. It is about thriving. Sur-thriving. Life presents us with traumas and life presents us with tragedies. Living on the planet in the third dimension is about us learning to handle these situations and better manage ourselves in the face of our challenges."

She goes on to offer, "We always have a choice. Live in fear and chaos or live in personal power and find positive solutions."

Luckett is right. No one is exempt from heartache. Sure, some is worse than others. But everyone endures a degree of suffering. Everyone. What is not universally shared, however, is the response. For some, the weight of a setback is too much, and they allow it to pull them further down.

Don't let that be you. Stare down setbacks. Learn from them. Resolve to have them push you forward. In Luckett's words, Sur-Thrive.

-76-
The Holy Grail of Success

What is key to success? A keen understanding of the technical ins and outs of your industry, product, or service? Sure. This is important, but not necessarily key. Hard work? Yes, this is important, but again not key. A strong network? Again, not key, but important.

So, what is key to success? Simple. Having purpose and meaning to whatever you do. Seriously! Think about it. It's purpose and meaning that drive you to be a student of your craft.

And without these foundational pieces, there is no way you can be committed enough to put in the necessary work, as well as to drive over those rough patches you'll encounter on the path to success.

It's the meaning and purpose that ignites the passion in you. And it's that energy that inspires legions of people to want to associate with you.

Vocational acumen, hard work and a network are all important. But isn't purpose and meaning the Holy Grail of success?

-77-
The Sub-Four-Minute Lesson

Prior to May 1954, experts from the athletic, medical, and scientific communities regarded running a sub-four-minute mile as an insurmountable limitation of the human body. In short, it could not be done. As such, runners came close to, but never surpassed this perceived physical limitation.

Then on May 6, 1954, in less-than-optimal conditions on an old cinder track near Oxford England, British runner Dr. Roger Bannister ran a mile in three minutes, fifty-nine-point-four seconds. Thereafter, world class runner after runner began running sub-four-minute miles.

History is made of men and women setting out and doing things that others said could not be done. Crossing oceans. Leading revolutions. Making scientific breakthroughs. Breaking down barriers. And the list could go on.

With each accomplishment, a statement is made. And it's the same statement: Do not allow the beliefs of others to alter the beliefs you have for yourself. As Dr. Roger Bannister demonstrated in less than four minutes, what matters most is what you believe.

-78-
Action To Create Value

Author, speaker, and personal development influencer Lewis Howes remarked in his book *The School of Greatness*, “Anyone can tell themselves they have a vision for what they want to create in the world, but it is our actions that dictate what we create in reality, where anything can and does happen.”

As Howes goes on to imply, the only thing carrying less value than talk is daydreaming. There is little value in sitting there and pondering a brighter future. It really doesn’t matter how glorious of a picture you paint in your mind. Oh sure, you can fool yourself into thinking that this picture creates value, but it really doesn’t.

Sure, a clear vision is important – and you should have one. But the real value doesn’t manifest itself – no matter how much clarity you might have – until you take some action. Any action. It is this action that creates something tangible that someone can assign value to.

-79-
The Accountability Loop

It's easy to be a victim. You know, where every setback in your life is followed by blaming others, complaining about circumstances, or denying that you could have had any responsibility. Yes, being the victim is easy. The problem is that few people want to associate with those who exhibit this behavior. And the ones who do, you want no part of. Being a victim is easy.

What is not easy is taking the tougher path and cutting this victim mindset out of your life. If you do, you will automatically begin to shift into the accountability loop where you take 100% responsibility for your life.

Here, you visualize a greater potential for your life. You take control of your actions and the circumstances that surround them. You create the conditions that you want or simply accept the ones you get. And you own any potential shortcomings.

As you do this, you not only attract like-minded people into your world, but you subconsciously seek them out. And this fuels even greater success.

-80-
Practice Makes Confidence

Have you ever wondered how some people present impeccable 30-second commercials or elevator speeches? They do a remarkable job sharing who they are, what they do, and how you might help them. You're envious, right?

The secret to this amazing short monologue is practice. In preparation for the flawless pitch you heard, the speaker likely spent some time in advance thinking through what they wanted to convey and drafting it. Then they tried it out in front of the mirror or maybe to some trusted friends or family. Next, they tweaked some words to help the audible flow.

Once they're satisfied, they recite it aloud when they have idle time. And they've let it play in their head - envisioning how it sounds and where the inflections work best.

The point is that by the time you heard it, the statement had been gone over dozens of times. And, no, all this practice doesn't make it perfect. What it does give them the confidence to deliver it in the flawless manner you heard.

-81-
Focus On Similarities

In his book *No One Gets There Alone*, mental edge guru and sports psychologist Dr. Rob Bell shares: "We have more in common with one another than we do differences. But we also focus on the differences more."

Bell shares that when we focus on the differences, we step into comparison mode. And it is here that we default to a scarcity mindset, which leads to fear, lack of confidence and isolation. It's a negative cycle.

He then talks about the opposite, saying: "When we focus on the similarities between us rather than the differences, we empathize, we care, we relate, we connect, we cooperate, we help, we humanize each other. We then see how our own experiences can benefit others."

So, whenever you are in a conversation, listen for the things you have in common. Kids. Love of sports. That boss that leaves you scratching your head. Whatever it might be. As Bell indicates that will naturally draw you closer to the person.

-82-
Long, Straight Drives

Whether or not you golf, you probably understand the game. You know that golf is not about putting a tiny, white ball six inches into a hole. Rather golf is about driving, shooting, and chipping that tiny, white ball hundreds of yards so that you are in the best position to putt it a short distance into the hole.

To be successful with networking, you need to approach it in a similar way. Networking is not about connecting with a stranger for the purpose of achieving your sales quota. In golfing terms, that would be like sinking that tiny, white ball in the hole from hundreds of yards away. How many golfers achieve that feat?

Rather, networking is about connecting with that stranger. Then understanding and helping them so that they become a friend. And then, in time, that friend refers you to the people, information, and opportunities that help you.

Thus, like golf, the focus of networking is not on the end result. It's on doing well with all the things leading up to the end result.

-83-
Savor Positive Emotions

Happiness coach and positive psychology expert Dr. John Schinnerer posed this question in his newsletter and on his blog: "Why do positive emotions exist?" He went on to refine his query by asking, "In other words, if traits are selected by evolution to continue in a species, why would positive emotions be selected? What purpose do they serve?"

Schinnerer goes on to answer these questions via the work of Dr. Barbara Fredrickson of the University of North Carolina. She concluded that positive emotions allow you to stretch your imagination as well as become more resilient in the face of adversity.

In short, positive emotions are vital to a healthy existence. But unlike, vigorous exercise (which also leads to good health), positive emotions – such love, hope, awe, happiness, curiosity, pride, contentment, and passion – allow you to enjoy the experience in the moment. So, find ways to have and savor positive emotions.

-84-
Crickets, Cowboys, And Commodities

In his book *The Science of Customer Connections: Manage Your Message to Grow Your Business*, marketing communication and buyer behavior strategist Jim Karrh shares three messaging pitfalls which he respectively dubs *crickets, cowboys,* and *commodities*.

Crickets is the situation where, for some reason, no one is sharing your message.

Cowboys is the situations where lots of people are sharing your message, but everyone has a different version of what the message is.
Commodities is the situation where there is a consistent message being shared, but the message is so littered with vague words and phrases that no one is quite certain what the message is.

As you work to educate your network about who you are, what you do and who you serve, keep Karrh's communication "fails" in mind. Afterall, a key to getting your network to effectively serve you is to teach them well enough about all the things you do so that they can speak on your behalf when you're not around.

-85-
The Value of Blinking

Blinking! What an amazing thing. The human body blinks every five or six seconds to help keep the eyes clean and vision clear. And it does this with lightning speed. Powered by the fastest muscle in the body, an average blink lasts only a mere 125 milliseconds. But do you know what? As amazing as blinking is, it has no external value. Why? Because every vision-enabled person on the planet can blink.

You see, value comes from doing things that others either cannot do or are unwilling to do. Think about it. Most people cannot consistently throw a 90 mile-per-hour fastball with relative precision. Hence, major league baseball pitchers are well paid for the value they bring to the game.

While you might not be an aspiring professional athlete, you are no doubt aspiring to success. And part of achieving success is creating value.

So, don't look to create value doing what's easy or what everyone else is doing. Rather, create value being unique and serving the world in a way that few others are.

-86-
Moment to Moment

In his book *Be Connected: Strategies To Attract the Right Opportunities, Connections and Clients Through Effective Networking*, professional speaker and social architect Terry Bean shared:

> "Life is nothing more than a bunch of moments. Each one gives you the opportunity to completely rebuild who you are. Don't carry your bad self into the next moment. Continually live each moment and make it the best it can be. When you take this moment-by-moment philosophy, you will be empowered to not be so connected to the bad. If negativity happens in one moment, then you acknowledge it and leave it there."

As Bean goes on to imply, this "leaving the negative behind" approach will help ensure that you are not stuck in a cycle of undesirable results. And when you are not attracting negative in your life, your mindset positions you to attract more of what you are looking for.

-87-
A Gift That Keeps Giving

As professional speaker and word of mouth referral consultant Matt Ward shares in his book *MORE: Word of Mouth Referrals, Lifelong Customers and Raving Fans*:

> "Each of us sits on a goldmine of potential connections. We all have networks that can be tapped to propel our contacts to the next level. What's missing is the method by which to link people up. Sure, we have LinkedIn, but those connections are lacking a personal touch. That's where you come into the picture."

Ward goes on to encourage you to connect the people you know via introductions. The connection will be beneficial to both contacts and you. Plus, he shares, that "Being a connector helps build deep and fulfilling relationships. When people discover they can come to you to get connected to others and to find resources they need, you will be in high demand." From that standpoint, Ward indicates, "building networks is a gift that keeps on giving."

-88-
Words, Tone, And Spacing

Take a moment and think of your favorite song. What do you like about it? The lyrics? Or maybe it's the music? Or perhaps it's the spacing between each. Chances are it's a combination of all. After all, it's hard to imagine that song – or any song – with only one of those components. It's the combination that makes it special.

The same is true with listening to others. To effectively tune into others, you need to listen to more than the words communicated. In addition to the words, you must also be attuned to the tone with which they are said. Likewise, the spacing between the words and tone helps provide meaning. After all, any message is not merely words. So, you need to listen not only for the content of the message, but for the intent, as well.

So, like your favorite song, to truly appreciate an entire message, you need to gather in a complete interplay of the words, tone and spacing.

-89-
Contributing Content On Social Media

To successfully make connections and build relationships using social media you need to – well – use social media. Add value, right? After all, you can't just create a profile on whatever platform and expect things to happen. An effective use for social media is to add value by contributing content.

Think for a moment about how you conduct yourself at a traditional networking event. You talk with people. You start discussions and you contribute to discussions that others have started. You answer questions and you ask questions that you hope others will be able to answer. Social media provides these same opportunities.

This does NOT mean pitch yourself or your product. It means provide information, insight, or opinions. Offer a solution to a problem. Share your experience as it relates to the discussion.

Remember, people want to associate with those who add value. On social media, contributing content will do that for you.

-90-
Stay Top of Heart

In the book *Becoming Competition Proof: Stand Out and Overcome Competition Through Generosity, Service and Added Value*, author, and adventure coach Berta Medina-Garcia shares:

> "I'm obsessed with mutual introductions. They are the greatest gift you can give a businessperson. It's a versatile tool. With a mutually beneficial introduction, you serve both people you are introducing, you add value to their lives, you practice generosity, and you stay top-of-heart."

Medina-Garcia is right. The singular act of connecting others results in two people who are appreciative of your efforts. Forevermore, when they interact these people will credit you with enriching their lives through your introduction.

The most beautiful thing is that you have an almost endless reservoir of opportunity to connect people. After all, when someone new enters your life, you can commence introducing them to the great people you already know. And everyone then has a new reason to keep you top-of-heart.

-91-
Be a Good Sport

Sportsmanship is not limited to games played on fields, courts, and courses. After all, what is sport? It is simply athletic competition. Absent the athletic, it is merely competition.

And as a human being, you compete every day. In your career. In business. At home, subtly, with neighbors. The entire human existence – like it or not – is about competing. Every day is about fighting to gain new ground. And every day is about keeping the ground you already have. Life is competition.

And any time there is competition, there are winners and losers. And there is achievement and disappointment. Thus, the practice of sportsmanship is vital to your everyday existence.

When you exhibit good sportsmanship, you set a wonderful example that elevates your brand. Others are proud to know you. They cannot help but like you. Moreover, they want to believe that they can trust you. So, whether you win or lose – at whatever – be sure to carry yourself with dignity and respect.

-92-
Winning By Taking Second

In 2012, during a cross country race in Burlada, Ivan Frenandez Anaya, an up-and-coming runner for Spain, was firmly in second place. No one behind him was even close.

Well ahead of him for most of the race was a Kenyan runner named Abel Mutai. Mutai was sure to be the victor. However, towards the end of the race the Kenyan thought he had finished the race and began to slow down. For whatever reason - fatigue or confusion - he had mistaken where the finish line was.

This allowed the Spanish runner, Anaya, to close the distance between second and first place. However, as he caught up with the mistaken Kenyan, he realized the situation. Rather than taking advantage of the situation, he slowed down and ushered Mutai across the true finish line first. In so doing, the Spaniard was celebrated as a champion of sportsmanship.

Do the right thing, no matter the cost. In the end, you win.

-93-
A Lesson From AA

In his book *No One Gets There Alone*, sports psychologist Dr. Rob Bell becomes vulnerable and shares about his own struggles with addiction and recovery. In so doing, he shares some aspects of the Alcoholics Anonymous program.

"The entire organization of Alcoholics Anonymous is about helping other alcoholics achieve sobriety and recovery. ... Alcoholics know that recovery depends upon having a sponsor. A sponsor is someone who can help another alcoholic and has gone through the process of recovery. Sponsors actually remain sober and recover by helping another person achieve sobriety. They give away the gifts of recovery so that they can keep it."

The point is this, while you might not have overcome an addiction, you have overcome other things. You've likely had moments of self-doubt. You've battled a competitive business environment. You've overcome the naysayers around you.

Whatever it is, you've worked through challenges and are better for it. Now, take a lesson from AA and help another through it too.

-94-
A Solid Foundation of Precious Things

Award-winning author and one of "America's Top 100 Thought Leaders", Frank Sonnenberg shared in an April 2020 tweet:

"Some of the most precious things you possess are your honor, your dignity, and your reputation. Be the person others look up to — whose character is beyond reproach. Be the one who inspires others to achieve excellence. And be the one who lives with honor and dignity. At the end of the day, if you're not proud of who you are and the way you chose to live your life, little else matters."

Sonnenberg shares an inspiring vision of what to aspire to. And this tweet leads to an article where he further encourages you to maintain willpower and not give into temptation. He encourages you to maintain a high standard, despite what the crowd might be doing. And never exhibit inappropriate behavior.

Yes, dignity and honor are precious things, but they are also the solid foundation upon which a great life is built.

-95-
Polite Or Honest

Organizational psychologist, author, and Wharton School of Business professor Dr. Adam Grant shared on Twitter that:

"When you're torn between being polite and being honest, err on the side of sincerity. It's better to be disliked but respected than to be liked but disrespected. In the long run, the people we trust the most are those with the courage to tell the truth."

While Grant's insight might make you uncomfortable, if you think about it, it has lots of merit. Yes, hearing the truth can hurt. But the truth – delivered in a caring and respectful way – leaves you with the potential for growth and improvement.

And sure, you might need some time to shake off the sting of learning how you're not perfect. But if you have the courage to accept the truth, you can begin taking steps to move yourself closer to perfection. So, when you ask for feedback, seek honesty, and let those who will settle for mediocrity take the politeness.

-96-
We Are All One

In his book *Be Connected: Strategies To Attract The Right Opportunities, Connections and Clients Through Effective Networking*, social architect Terry Bean shares:

"So many people talk about the idea of six degrees of separation. Stop it! We don't need to focus on being separate. We are separate enough. Consider the degree of connectedness we have.

"When we take heed of our connectedness, we are more likely to want to help one another. We also become more comfortable with asking for the help we need."

Bean goes on to share that the essence of networking is really the essence of life. We are here to support one another. He makes the point that we are all one. And that we are all working to eliminate pain in the lives of others. And that if you focus on helping others, you are really helping yourself.

So, look around. There are people to help. Take action. And that action will serve you in the end, too.

-97-
Create Networking Bonds

Think about it. What did you do that last time you were at an event, and someone jumped right in and started talking "Brass Tacks"? "Who does your printing? Are you happy? I can do better. Give me a chance. Throw me some business. Well, why not?"

Did you do business with them? Not likely. Chances are when you hit it off with someone at an that event, the encounter started with small talk.

As an analogy, "small talk" is like the warmup you do before you get into the work out. It is the foundation of the "knowing" in "Know, Like & Trust.

It is also the foundation upon which people come to like you. In fact, social science and brain studies have shown that in the few minutes where chitchat is happening, people even start to formulate a sense as to whether or not they trust you.

In short, small talk creates networking bonds. So, make this chitchat a part of your networking game plan.

-98-
Let Freedom Ring

As you likely know, the 4th of July is a national holiday in the United States. It's a day of parades, gatherings, and fireworks. It marks the annual celebration of independence for this country. And if you call yourself an American, it should be a wonderful day for you.

Unfortunately, we often take our way of life for granted. The ability to cast a vote. The right to speak our minds. The opportunity to pursue a professional endeavor of our own choosing.

While the 4th of July is the annual celebration of our nation's independence, everyday should be a celebration of your right to do what you do. And every day should be devoted to helping others find their American Dream, however they choose to define it.

So, certainly enjoy the 4th of July every year when it comes around. But know that doing what you do (and helping others do what they do) is something that allows freedom to ring
365 days a year.

-99-
Stop Drinking In The Desert

In her book *The Light in 9/11: Shocked by Kindness, Healed by Love*, author Lisa Luckett shared an insightful story. In working through the hurt and unanswered questions following the tragic loss of her husband in the Twin Towers on September 11th, Luckett's therapist asked "Why are you going to the desert for a drink of water?

Luckett shares that from that simple question she learned to steer away from people who were unbalanced, unsupportive, or judgmental regardless of her previous relationship to them. She goes on to explain that you need to build into your life people who are as eager to support you as you are to serve them. In her words, "If someone caused me self-doubt or if I felt unjustly criticized by them, I stepped aside."

The reality is that you add value to others. And somehow, they should add value to you. If not, they are merely a desert where you will never find a drink.

-100-
Doers v. Dreamers

Steve Jobs, American business icon, technology innovator, and founder of Apple Computer, once remarked:

"Most people never pick up the phone and call. Most people never ask. And that's what separates, **the people that do things** from the people that just dream about them."

Which are you? A doer? Or just a dreamer? Sure, there is value in devoting time to envisioning a better day. In fact, it might be something great. But if that's all it is – idle pondering of something you have no intention of reaching for – then you're just a dreamer.

Don't settle for that. Be a doer. Pick up the phone and call. Ask for what you need. Roll up your sleeves (literally and figuratively) and take steps to make your dreams a reality. There is not guarantee that it will happen. But without any action at all, you're guaranteed that it won't.

-101-
I Love You. Period.

In their book *The Go-Giver Marriage: A Little Story About the 5-Secrets of Lasting Love* authors John David Mann and Ana Gabriel Mann indicate that the four deadliest words in any marriage are, "I love you, but ..." They go on to share that love is unconditional and that you accept that special someone, for better or for worse.

Sure, only one person in your network might rise to the level of being a spouse or significant other. Nevertheless, you still have relationships with the people around you. And thus the sentiment of The Go-Giver Marriage authors is the same. No one is perfect. Everyone has shortcomings. Care about them unconditionally.

Not everyone is organized or always on time. Not everyone shares your religion or political leaning. Not everyone shares your hobbies and interests. They are all, however, human. As such, they need your support as if you're saying: I love you. Period.

There you have it—101 essays. But we wanted to offer a bonus essay. Before we do, if you're interested in exploring other books, content, and programs by Frank Agin, visit frankagin.com or simply search "Frank Agin" on whatever platform you use to get great content.

-102-
Share A Pizza; Build a Friendship

In a 2017 study out of the University of Chicago, researchers found that when people eat the same food, they're more likely to co-operate better and resolve conflict faster.

According to a co-author of the study – which was called *A recipe for friendship: Similar food consumption promotes trust and co-operation* – "When people eat the same food, they feel closer and then are more trusting of another person."

While you might not be keen on ordering the same thing as your lunch partner, there seems to be real power in breaking bread with those in your network.

Face it. Life is full of disagreements, difficult conversations, and conflicting interests. And while a simple meal won't make it go away, the act of sitting together to eat can serve to open the lines of communication. And that might just be the inroad you need.

So, the lesson is this: Share a pizza; Build a friendship.

About The Author

Frank Agin is president of AmSpirit Business Connections, which empowers entrepreneurs, sales representatives, and professionals to become successful and gain more referrals through networking.

He also shares information and insights on professional relationships, business networking and best practices for generating referrals on his Networking Rx podcast and through various professional programs.

Finally, Frank is the author of several books, including *Foundational Networking: Building Know, Like & Trust to Create a Life of Extraordinary Success*. See all his books and programs at frankagin.com. You can reach him at frankagin@amspirit.com.

www.ingramcontent.com/pod-product-compliance
Lightning Source LLC
Chambersburg PA
CBHW040757220326
41597CB00029BB/4971
* 9 7 8 1 9 6 7 5 2 1 2 0 3 *